Victory in Jesus

Favorite Hymns and Gospel Songs

Arranged for Choir and Congregation

TOM FETTKE

Kansas City, MO 64141

Victory in Jesus

Words and Music by
EUGENE M. BARTLETT
Arranged by Tom Fettke

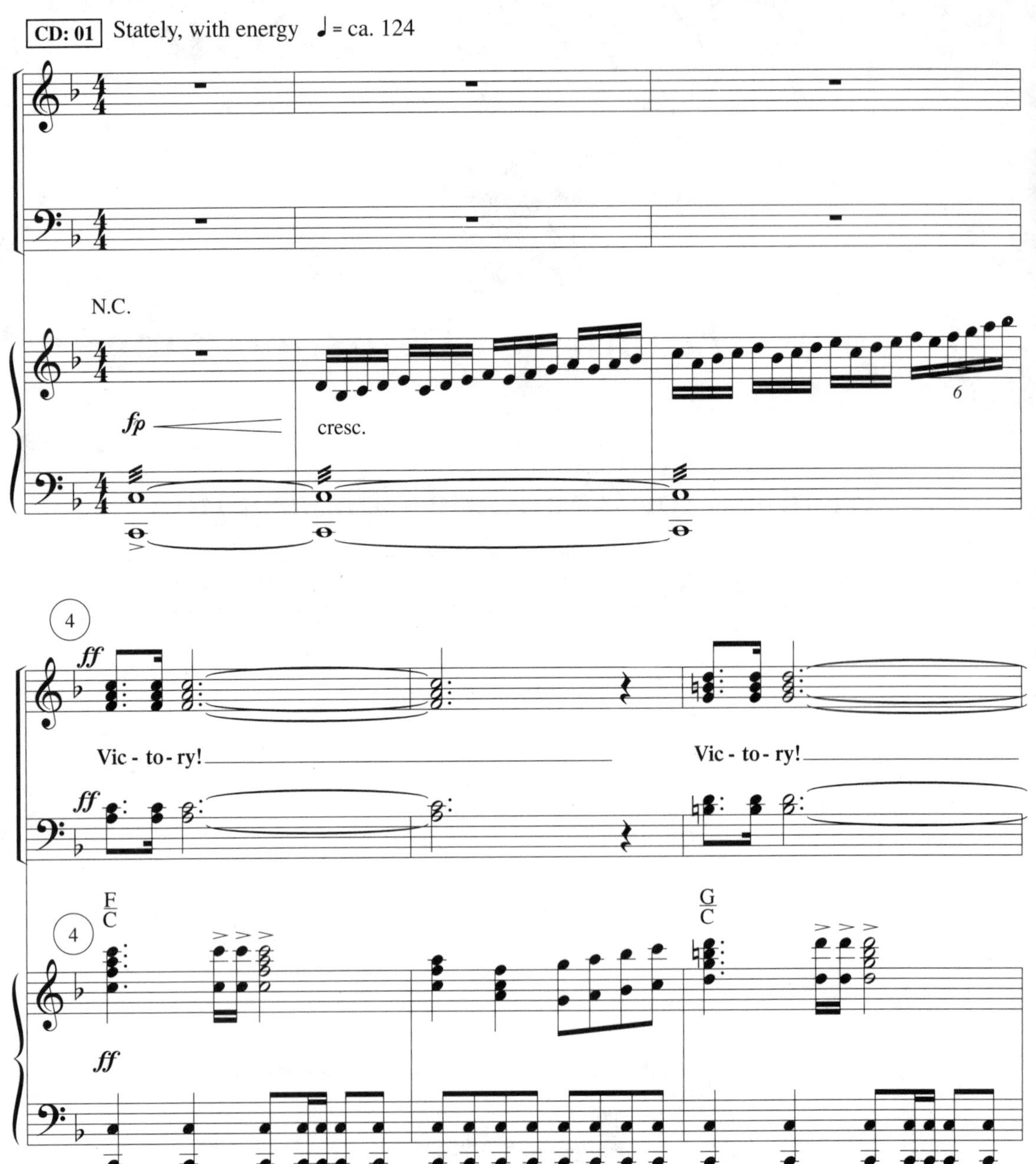

8
Vic-to-ry!
Vic-to-ry in
G/C
A♭/C
B♭/C
CD: 02
Gospel Swing and
mf Unison
Je - sus!
I
C
C/B♭
F2/A
F/A
Gm7
Gm7/C
Swing eighths
decresc.
13
heard an old, old sto-ry, how a Sav-ior came from
F
F6
Gm/F
F
Gm/F
B♭/F
mf

17
glo - ry, How He gave His life on Cal - va - ry to
B♭/F F Dm7 C F Dm7
17
save a wretch like me. I heard a - bout His
21
G7 G/D G9 C B♭/C F
21
groan - ing, of His pre - cious blood's a - ton - ing. Then
Gm/F F Gm/F B♭/F B♭/F F F/E

25
CD: 03
I re - pent - ed of my sins and won the vic - to -
Dm
B♭m6
D♭
F
C
A7
C♯
Dm
Gm7
B♭
C
C7
ry. O vic - to - ry in Je - sus, my
f Divisi
29
F
B♭
F
F
F7
f
Sav - ior for - ev - er! He sought me and
33
B♭6
B♭
B♭
D
F
Dm
B♭m6
D♭

bought me with His re - deem - ing blood. He
F/C
F6
F
G9
G13
G9
C7
B♭/C
C13
37
loved me ere I knew Him, and all my love is
F
B♭/F
F
F7
B♭6
B♭
due Him. He plunged me to vic - to - ry be -
41
B♭/F
F
F/E
Dm
Am7
Dm7

44
Even eighths
rit.
CD: 04
neath the cleans - ing flood.
Gm9 Gm B♭/C C7
F
E♭M7/F E♭/F
mf
Even eighths
rit.
Low voice solo
mp
48
Slowly, with warmth ♩= ca. 78
I heard a - bout His
F/B♭ Gm9 B♭/E♭ E♭2/F
B♭2 F/B♭ B♭
mp
heal - ing, of His cleans-ing pow'r re - veal - ing, How He
A♭/B♭ B♭13 E9♭5 E♭6 E♭ Cm7 Cm7/F Fsus F7

52
made the lame to walk a - gain and caused the blind to
Gm9 Gm Gm(M7) Gm7 B♭6/C C7sus C9
rit. Duet 56 a tempo
see. And then I cried, "Dear Je - sus, come and
mel. mp
Fsus F/E♭ Dsus D G F/G G G7
rit. a tempo
60
heal my bro - ken spir - it;" And some - how Je - sus
C C/G G D/F♯ Em Cm6/E♭

CD: 05
Gospel Swing and =
came and brought to me the vic - to - ry.
G/D B7/D♯ Em Em7 Am7 C/D D7 G Am/G GM7 Am/G
Swing eighths
mf
Choir
mf Unison
65
I heard a - bout a man - sion He has
mf Unison
GM7 C/G C/D C2/D
G GM7/D G7
69
built for me in glo - ry, And I heard a - bout the
Am/G C/G C/G G G/F♯ Em D

streets of gold be - yond the crys - tal sea; A -

G Em7 A7 A/E A9 D7 C/D

(73)

bout the an - gels sing - ing, and the old re - demp - tion

(73) G Am/G G G7 C6 C

sto - ry; And (77) some sweet day I'll sing up there the

C/G G G/F♯ (77) Em Cm6/E♭ G/D B7/D♯ Em Em7

CD: 06
Gospel 2-beat feel
f Divisi
song of vic - to - ry.
O
f Divisi
Am7 C/D D7 G C/G G C/G G Am/G G
gliss.
82
vic - to - ry in Je - sus, my Sav - ior for -
82
G C/G G G7 C6 C C/E
f Even eighths
86
ev - er! He sought me and bought me with
C/G G
86
Em Cm6/E♭ G/D G

90
His re - deem - ing blood. He loved me ere I
A9 A6 A9 D7 D13
90
G C/D
knew Him, and all my love is due Him. He
G G7 C6 C C/G G G/F♯
94
CD: 07
plunged me to vic - to - ry be - neath the cleans - ing
94
Em Bm Em7 Am9 Am Am7/D D7

99
ff
flood.
Vic - to - ry in
G C/G G G/F D♭/E♭ E♭ Fm/E♭ E♭9
A♭ D♭/A♭
Je - sus, my Sav - ior for - ev - er! He
A♭ A♭7 D♭6 D♭ D♭/F D♭/A♭ A♭
103
sought me and bought me with His re - deem - ing
Fm D♭m6/F♭ A♭/E♭ A♭ B♭9 B♭6 B♭9

107
blood. He loved me ere I knew Him, and
E♭7 E♭13 A♭ D♭/E♭ A♭ A♭7
all my love is due Him. He plunged me to
111
D♭6 D♭ D♭/A♭ A♭ A♭/G F m
CD: 08
vic - to - ry be - neath the cleans - ing flood.
C m F m7 B♭m9 B♭m D♭/E♭ E♭7 A♭ D♭/A♭

116

Vic - to - ry! ___

A♭ D♭/E♭ 116 A♭ B♭m/A♭ A♭ D♭/A♭ Cm/A♭

120

Vic - to - ry! ___ Vic - to - ry!

B♭/A♭ A♭ B♭/A♭ Cm/A♭ B♭/A♭ 120 C♭/G♭

Vic - to - ry in Je - sus! ___

D♭/E♭ A♭ N.C. A♭ 8va

Wonderful, Wonderful Jesus

with

O How I Love Jesus

Arranged by Tom Fettke

*Arr. © 1997 Birdwing Music. All rights administered by EMI Christian Music Publishing, PO Box 5085, Brentwood, TN 37024. All rights reserved. Used by permission.

CD: 11
Je - sus Will some - where find a song.
G/B G Em7 F♯m7 Bm Em7 F♯m/A A7 Dsus D
22
Divisi
mf
Won-der-ful, won-der-ful Je - sus, In the heart He im-plant-eth a
22 G Am/G G G/B G6/B B♭°7 Am7 D7 D9
26
song: A song of de-liv-'rance, of cour-age, of strength; In the
G2 G D7/A 26 G/B Dsus D D/C G/B G G/F C/E Cm/E♭

CD: 12
f Unison
heart He im-plant-eth a song.
There is
f Unison
G/D
B♭°/D
A m7/D
D 7
G
E♭/G
31
More intensely
nev - er a cross so heav - y,
There is
A♭2
A♭
E♭7sus/B♭
E♭7/B♭
A♭2/C
A♭/C
f
nev - er a weight of woe,
But that
D♭2
D♭
F sus/C
F
B♭sus
B♭m

35
Je - sus will help to car - ry Be -
35 E♭7 D♭/E♭ E♭ A♭2/C A♭ Fm7
CD: 13
39 Flowing
cause He loves you so.
Won - der - ful, won - der - ful
Gm7 Cm7 Fm7 Gm/B♭ B♭7 E♭sus E♭
39 A♭ A♭/C B°7
Je - sus, In the heart He im - plant - eth a song: A
B♭m7 E♭7 B♭m7 E♭ A♭2 A♭ E♭7/B♭

43
Divisi
song of de - liv - 'rance, of courage, of strength; In the
Divisi
Ab/C Ab2/C Ab/C Ebsus Eb Eb/Db Ab/C Ab Ab/Gb Db/F Dbm/Fb
43
CD: 14
rit.
heart He im - plant - eth a song.
Ab/Eb B°7/Eb Bbm7/Eb Eb7 Ab Ab7sus Ab7
decresc.
rit.
48
Warmly, slower ♪ = ca. 76
mp Unison
O how I love Je - sus, O how I love
mp Unison
48
Db Db° Db Db/F E°7 Ebm7 Ab7 Gb/Ab Ab7
mp

52
mf
Je - sus, O how I love Je - sus, Be -
mf
Divisi
D♭2 D♭ D♭/F A♭7/E♭ D♭ F F/A B♭m D♭7/A♭ D♭7
52
mf
Divisi
56
cause He first loved me.
E♭m/G♭ B♭/F E♭m7 Fm/A♭ A♭7 D♭sus D♭ D♭sus/A♭
56
mp
mp
(10)
Je - sus.
mp
D♭sus/A♭
D♭2 D♭

His Eye Is on the Sparrow

with

God Leads Us Along

Arranged by Tom Fettke

Flowing, in 6 ♪ = ca. 108

CD: 15

N.C. C C/B♭ F/A Fm/A♭

mf slight rit.

mf Unison

In

mf Unison

C/G G13 G7 C2 FM7 C2 FM7

a tempo

6 *"God Leads Us Along (G. A. Young)

shad - y green pas- tures so rich and so sweet, God leads His dear chil- dren a -

6 C2 FM7 Em7 Am7 Dm7 Dm7/G G7

10

long. Where the wa - ter's cool flow bathes the wea - ry one's feet, God

C FM7 C2 FM7 Em Am

10

CD: 16

leads His dear chil - dren a - long.

14 Stronger

Divisi

Some thro' the wa - ters,

Divisi

Dm7 Dm7/G Em/G Dm7/G C C C/E

14

some thro' the flood, Some thro' the fire, but all thro' the blood.

F Dm7 G7sus G7 G7/F Em7 Am7 D9 G7sus G7

18
CD: 17
Some thro' great sor - row, but God gives a song In the night sea - son and
18
C2 Em7 F2 C C/D Em7 Am7
*"His Eye Is On the Sparrow" (Martin/Gabriel)
22
New tempo - in 2 ♩. = ca. 44
Solo
mf
Why should I feel dis - cour - aged?
rit.
all the day long.
Dm7 G7 C
22
C2
C2 C C2 C Csus/D C7/E
rit.

26

Why should the shad - ows come? Why should my heart be

F C $\frac{C^9}{B\flat}$ 26 A 7 $\frac{A^7}{C\sharp}$

lone - ly And long for heav'n and home When

D $^4_2$ Dm Dm7 G 7 $\frac{G^2}{B}$ $\frac{G}{B}$ C 2

30
Je - sus is my por- tion? My con - stant Friend is
mp
Oo Oo
mp
C G7sus/D G7/D C2/E
He. His eye is on the spar - row, And I
34
Ah
F A7/E Dm G7 G/F C2/E C/E G7/D C C♯°7

38
know He watch - es me. His eye is on the
Ah Ah
Dm7(4) G7 C G7/D C2/E C/E B♭/C C7
38
CD: 18
Soloist joins choir
spar-row, And I know He watch-es me.
Ah I
f
F Fm/D C/G G7 F/C C

42
sing be - cause I'm hap - py, I sing be - cause I'm
G
G/F
C/E
C
G
f
free; For His eye is on the spar - row, And I
46
C
C/E
Dm7
C
Dm7
C7/E
F
Fm6
CD: 19
know He watch - es me.
C/G
G7
C
C/B♭
A♭7

51
mp
"Let not your heart be trou - bled," His ten - der word I
mp
51
D♭
E♭m/D♭
D♭9
G♭
mp
hear; And rest - ing on His good - ness,
55
D♭
A♭m6/C♭
B♭9
B♭/D
E♭2 4
E♭m
E♭m7
mf
59
I lose my doubt and fear. Tho' by the path He
A♭7
A♭/C
D♭2
mf

leadeth But one step I may see, His
A♭7sus/E♭
A♭7/E♭
D♭2/F
G♭
B♭7/F
E♭m
63
eye is on the sparrow, And I know He watches
A♭7
A♭/G♭
D♭2/F
D♭/F
E♭m7
D♭
D°7
E♭m7(4)
A♭7
67
CD: 20
me. His eye is on the sparrow, And I
D♭
A♭7/E♭
D♭2/F
D♭/F
G♭
G♭m6/E♭

f
71
know He watch-es me. I sing be-cause I'm
D♭/A♭
A♭7
D♭
A♭
A♭/G♭
hap-py, I sing be-cause I'm free; For His
D♭/F
D♭
A♭
D♭
75
eye is on the spar-row, And I know He watch-es
D♭/F
E♭m7
D♭
E♭m7
D♭7/F
G♭
G♭m6
D♭/A♭
A♭7

(79)

me. For His eye is on the sparrow, And I

D♭ D♭/F E♭m7 D♭ E♭m7 D♭7/F G♭ G♭m6

(83)

mf me, watch-es me, watch-es

me, watch-es me,

know He watch-es me, watch-es me, watch-es

mf

me, watch-es me,

D♭/A♭ A♭7 D♭ E♭m/D♭ D♭ G♭/D♭ D♭M7

mf

me, watch-es me.

rit. (5)

watch-es me, watch-es me.

me, watch-es me.

watch-es me, watch-es me.

G♭/D♭ D♭M7 G♭/D♭ D♭

8va

rit.

Blessed Be the Name

with

All Hail the Power of Jesus' Name

Arranged by Tom Fettke

Majestic ♩ = ca. 100

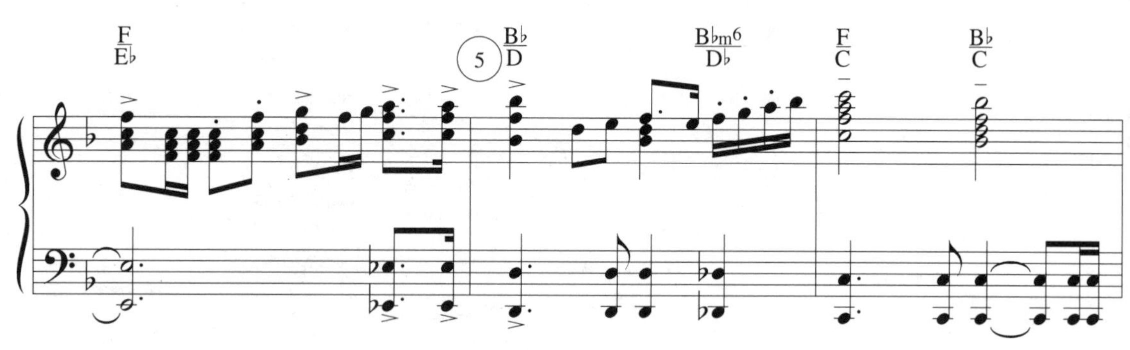

12
ff
Bless - ed be the name of the Lord!
ff
F/C
Dm/B
Gm7/C
12
ff
CD: 22
accel.
mf
O
C
B♭/C
accel. and decresc.
C
Gm/C Am/C B♭/C
C7
*"Blessed Be the Name" (Wesley, Hudson/Unknown)
16
Slightly faster ♩= ca. 108
for a thou - sand tongues to sing,
Bless-ed be the name of the
mf
16
F
March feel
mf
B♭/F
F
melody
F/A
B♭

20
Lord! The glo - ries of my God and King,
C7sus
C7
20
F
B♭/F
F
CD: 23
24
Unison
Bless-ed be the name of the Lord! Bless-ed be the name,
Unison
F/A
B♭
F/C
C7
F
B♭/F
24
F
Light 2-beat feel
F/A
Bless-ed be the name; Bless-ed be the name of the Lord!
B♭
F/A
C7/G
F
Dm7
G7
C7

*Arr. © 1997 Birdwing Music. All rights administered by EMI Christian Music Publishing, PO Box 5085, Brentwood, TN 37024. All rights reserved. Used by permission.

42
crown Him Lord of all. Bring forth the roy - al
G D/F♯ Em D/A A7 D D13 G G/B G
CD: 25
di - a - dem, And crown Him Lord of
D7 G/D D7 G/D D7 Em G/B C G/D Gsus/D D D7
47 Unison
all. Bless-ed be the name, Bless-ed be the name;
Unison
G C/D 47 G Light 2-beat feel G7 C G

51
Bless-ed be the name of the Lord!
Bless-ed be the name,
G
Em
Am7
D7
51
G
G7
CD: 26
Bless-ed be the name;
Bless-ed be the name of the Lord!
C
G
G
G/F♯
Em
Cm/E♭
G/D
D7
G
G/F
f Divisi
56
Let every kindred, every tribe On
f Divisi
E♭sus
D♭/E♭
E♭7
56
A♭
E♭7
Fm
E♭
A♭
f

60
this ter - res - trial ball To Him all maj - es -
E♭7 Fm A♭/E♭ E♭7 A♭ E♭ A♭/E♭ E♭(no 3rd) A♭/E♭
ty as - cribe, And crown Him Lord of
A♭/E♭ B♭m/E♭ A♭/E♭ E♭ A♭/E♭ E♭ A♭ E♭/G Fm E♭/B♭ B♭7
65
all. To Him all maj - es - ty as - cribe, And
E♭ D♭/E♭ E♭7 A♭ A♭/C A♭ E♭7 A♭/E♭ E♭7 A♭/E♭ E♭7 Fm

CD: 27
crown Him Lord of all.
A♭/C
D♭
A♭/E♭
A♭sus/E♭
E♭
E♭7
A♭
D♭/E♭
70
Unison
Bless-ed be the name, Bless-ed be the name; Bless-ed be the name of the
Unison
70
A♭
A♭7
D♭
A♭
Fm
74
CD: 28
Lord! Bless-ed be the name, Bless-ed be the name;
B♭m7
E♭7
74
A♭
D♭
A♭

Divisi
78
Bless-ed be the name of the Lord!
All hail the pow'r of
Divisi
A♭
A♭/G
Fm
D♭m/F♭
A♭/E♭
E♭
A♭
N.C.
78
A♭
ff
Je - sus' name.
Bless - ed be the name of the
ff
E♭
Fm
E♭
E♭/D♭
A♭/C
D♭
D♭6
A♭/E♭
E♭sus
E♭
ff
82
Lord.
82
N.C.
A♭/E♭
A♭
G♭
D♭/F
E♭sus
D♭/E♭
A♭

Just As I Am

CHARLOTTE ELLIOTT

WILLIAM B. BRADBURY
Arranged by Tom Fettke

*A keyboard guide is provided on the accompaniment trax.

**Or sing the complete selection A cappella. Decrease the amount of rest between measures 13 and 14.

8
CD: 31
2nd time
that Thou bidd'st me come to Thee, O
Thee whose blood can cleanse each spot, O
8
2nd time - Accompanied
CD: 30
1st time
1
Lamb of God, I come! I come! 2. Just
Lamb of God, I come! I
1
2
mf
come! 3. Just
mf
2
cresc.
mf

15
as I am, Thou wilt re - ceive, Wilt
15
wel - come, par - don, cleanse, re - lieve. Be -
19
cause Thy prom - ise I be - lieve, O
19

Lamb of God, I come! I
23
come! O Lamb of God, I
mp
23
come!
come, I come.
mp

There Is a Fountain

with

At the Cross

Glory to His Name

Arranged by Tom Fettke

Broadly ♩= ca. 72

CD: 32

E♭2 mp Cm7 mf A♭M7

*"There Is a Fountain" (Cowper/Traditional melody)

mp

6 Warmly

A cappella preferred

There is a foun - tain

B♭2

decresc.

6 Opt. accompaniment

N.C. B♭ E♭/B♭ B♭ B♭/D

mp

filled with blood Drawn from Im - man - uel's veins; And

E♭ B♭ Dm Gm C9 Fsus F B♭

10
sin - ners, plunged be - neath that flood, Lose all their guilt - y
10 B♭ B♭7sus B♭7 E♭ F9/E♭ B♭2/D B♭/D B♭ F/A Gm7 Cm N.C.
CD: 33
mf
14
stains; Lose all their guilt - y stains, Lose
B♭2
Accompanied
14
E♭/B♭
mp
mf
8vb
18
all their guilt - y stains. And sin - ners, plunged be -
B♭2 Fsus F B♭ B♭7sus B♭7
18

*Arr. © 1997 Birdwing Music. All rights administered by EMI Christian Music Publishing, PO Box 5085, Brentwood, TN 37024. All rights reserved. Used by permission.

CD: 35
mf Divisi
sa - cred head For sin - ners such as I? At the
mf Divisi
E♭
Fm
Fm7
B♭13
B♭7
E♭
31
With assurance
cross, at the cross where I first saw the light, And the bur - den of my heart rolled a -
31
E♭
Cm7
A♭/C
Cm7
Fm9
Fm
B♭7
Fm7
A♭/B♭
B♭
mf
35
way. It was there by faith I re - ceived my sight, And
E♭
35
A♭
E♭
G7/D
Cm
Cm7

*Arr. © 1997 Birdwing Music. All rights administered by EMI Christian Music Publishing, PO Box 5085, Brentwood, TN 37024. All rights reserved. Used by permission.

CD: 37
blood ap - plied, Glo - ry to His name.
C
G2/B
G/B
Gm/B♭
Am9
CM7/D
D7
G
G/F
E♭7
49
f Divisi
I am so won - drous-ly saved from sin; Je - sus so sweet - ly a -
f Divisi
49
A♭
A♭/C
D♭
B♭m7
E♭
E♭7
A♭
Fm7
f
bides with - in. There at the cross where He took me in–
53
B♭7
E♭7
53
A♭
A♭/C
D♭
D♭/F
A♭
3

CD: 38
57
Glo - ry to His name!
Glo - ry to His
A♭/E♭
Cm/E♭
E♭7
A♭
57
D♭
name!
Glo - ry to His name!
A♭
Fm7
B♭7
E♭
61
CD: 39
There to my heart was the blood ap - plied.
Glo - ry to His
61
A♭
A♭/C
D♭
D♭/F
A♭
3
A♭/E♭
Cm/E♭
E♭7

Optional descant

65

f

Glo-ry to His name!

f *Unison*

name! Glo - ry to His name!

f *Unison*

A♭ D♭ A♭

65

f

69

Glo-ry to His name! There to my heart was the

Glo - ry to His name! There to my heart was the

A♭ Fm7 B♭7 E♭ A♭ A♭/C

69

blood ap - plied, Glo-ry to His name!
blood ap - plied. Glo - ry to His name!
D♭ D♭/F A♭ A♭/E♭ Cm/E♭ E♭7 A♭
8vb
73 Divisi
cresc.
rit.
Glo - ry, glo - ry to His
Divisi
cresc.
B♭m/A♭ A♭M7 D♭/A♭ E♭/A♭
cresc.
rit.
ff
name!
ff
N.C. A♭2 A♭/G♭ E♭sus/F♭ A♭
ff

On Jordan's Stormy Banks

with

Shall We Gather at the River?
Come, Thou Fount of Every Blessing

Arranged by Tom Fettke

CD: 41
rit. e cresc.
Slower
rit.
In tempo ♩ = ca. 124
mf
Unison
riv - er That flows by the throne of God. On
Eb Eb9/Db C7 Fm7 Ab/Bb Gm/Bb Bb7 Ab/Eb Eb
15 * "On Jordan's Stormy Banks" (Stenett/Traditional melody)
Jor - dan's storm - y banks I stand And cast a wish - ful
Ab/Eb
19
Divisi
CD: 42
eye To Ca - naan's fair and hap - py land Where
Bbsus Bb Gm/Bb Bb7 Eb Bb7 Eb/G Ab6

Stronger
23
my pos - ses - sions lie.
I am bound for the prom - ised
land; I am bound for the prom - ised land.
O
27
who will come and go with me? I am bound for the prom - ised
Eb/Bb
Bb7sus
Bb7
Eb
Ebsus/F
Eb/G
Bb
Ab
Eb/Bb

30
CD: 43
land.
E♭
G
D
Em7
A7sus
A7
33
*"Come, Thou Fount of Every Blessing" (Robinson/Traditional American Melody)
mf Bright
Come, Thou Fount of ev - ery bless - ing, Tune my heart to
D
G
D
Em7
D
F♯
G
sing Thy grace. Streams of mer - cy, nev - er ceas - ing,
37
D
A
A7
D
D
G
D

CD: 44
Unison
Call for songs of loud - est praise. I am
Unison
D Em7 D/F♯ G D/A A7 D A A13 A7
42
Divisi
bound for the king-dom, will you go to glo-ry with me? Hal - le - lu - jah,
Divisi
D A D A7/E D/F♯ Em7 D/F♯ G
46
CD: 45
praise the Lord. Hal - le - lu - jah, praise the
D/A A7 D D/F♯ Em7 D/F♯ G D/A Asus A
cued notes optional

f Unison
50
Lord.
I am bound for the prom - ised
f Unison
D
D/A
f
land; I am bound for the prom - ised land. O
A7
D
A7/E
D/F♯
A
54
CD: 46
who will come and go with me? I am bound for the prom - ised
D
G6/D
D/F♯
G
D/A
A7sus
A7

58
Divisi
land. I am bound for the prom - ised land; I am
Divisi
D
D C
B♭7
58
E♭ B♭
B♭7
62
bound for the prom - ised land. O who will come and
E♭
B♭7 F
E♭ G
B♭
62
E♭
A♭6 E♭
CD: 47
go with me? I am bound for the prom - ised land.
E♭
E♭ G
A♭
E♭ B♭
B♭7sus
B♭7
E♭

66
Hal - le - lu - jah, praise the Lord. Hal - le - lu - jah,
E♭ Fm7 E♭/G A♭ E♭/B♭ B♭7 E♭ E♭ Fm7 E♭/G A♭
69
praise the Lord. Praise the
ff
E♭/B♭ B♭sus B♭ E♭ A♭/B♭
cued notes optional
72
Lord!
E♭
N.C.
8vb

I Surrender All

with

Spirit of the Living God

Arranged by Tom Fettke

CD: 49

liv - ing God, fall fresh on me.

Gm/F F B♭2/F C7/F F F9 E♭/F F7

13

mf *Divisi*

Melt me, mold me, fill me,

mf *Divisi*

13 B♭ Gm7 Am7 Dm7 G G/F

mf

17

mp

use ___ me. Spir - it of the liv - ing God,

mp

C/E Csus/D C 17 F2 FM7 F Gm/B♭ D7/A Gm

mp

CD: 50
rit.
a tempo
fall fresh on me.
F/C
B♭/C
C7
F
E♭/F
Dm/F
F7
rit.
a tempo
22
*"I Surrender All" (VanDeVenter/Weeden)
Unison
All to Je - sus I sur - ren - der; All to Him I
Unison
B♭
E♭/B♭
B♭
E♭6
F6
F/E♭
B♭2/D
B♭/D
B♭M7/D
E♭
B♭/D
26
free - ly give. I will ev - er love and trust Him,
Cm7
Dm/F
B♭
B♭2
B♭
E♭/B♭
B♭
Am7
D7

CD: 51
30
In His pres - ence dai - ly live. I sur - ren - der
Mel.
G m7 C m7 B♭/D E♭6 D m/F B♭
30
B♭ E♭/B♭ B♭
all. I sur - ren - der all.
C m7 F E♭/F D m/F C m/F B♭2 B♭
34
Divisi
Mel.
mf
All to Thee, my blessed Sav - ior, I sur - ren - der
Divisi
mf
34
B♭ E♭/B♭ B♭ F7sus/C B♭/D B♭M7/D F/E♭ E♭ B♭/F E♭/F D m/F F7
mf

mp
cresc. poco a poco
Unison
39
all.
O Je-sus cleanse me,
mp
Unison
B♭
39
A♭/B♭
mp
cresc. poco a poco
CD: 52
teach me, call me, lead me.
E♭/B♭
F/B♭
B♭
rit.
44
a tempo
f Divisi
I sur-ren-der all.
f Divisi
I sur-ren-der, I sur-ren-der all.
A♭/B♭
B♭7
44
E♭
B♭/E♭
A♭/E♭
E♭
B♭7
rit.
f a tempo

48
I sur-ren - der all. All to Thee, my
I sur-ren - der, I sur-ren-der all.
B♭7
A♭/B♭
Gm/B♭
Fm/B♭
E♭2
E♭
48
E♭
Fm/E♭
A♭/E♭
E♭
decresc.
rit.
bless - ed Sav - ior, I sur-ren - der all.
decresc.
E♭/G
E♭M7/G
A♭4/2
A♭
E♭/B♭
Fm/B♭
E♭/B♭
B♭7
E♭
E♭/D♭
A♭2/C
A♭/C
A♭m6/C♭
decresc.
rit.
53
mf decresc.
In tempo - slower
p
I sur-ren - der all.
mf decresc.
p
53
E♭/B♭
A♭/B♭
Gm/B♭
B♭7
In tempo - slower
E♭sus
E♭2
decresc.
mf
p

How Great Thou Art

with

I Sing the Mighty Power of God

Arr. by Tom Fettke and Bruce Greer

10
rit.
spread the flow - ing seas a - broad, And built the loft - y
B♭ F7/B♭ E♭/B♭ B♭ F7/C B♭2/D B♭/D E♭ Cm7 Fsus F
Slower tempo ♩ = ca. 72
14
CD: 54
skies.
B♭2 Cm/B♭ B♭
mf flowing
mp Divisi
17
*"How Great Thou Art" (Stuart K. Hine)
O Lord, my God, when I in awe-some
E♭/F F Fsus F B♭2 B♭ F7/C B♭/D E♭
mp

won - der Con - sid - er all the worlds Thy hands have
E♭ E°7 B♭/F Dm/F F9
made, I see the stars, I hear the roll - ing
21
B♭2 B♭ F Fsus F B♭ F7/C B♭/D E♭
CD: 55
thun - der, Thy pow'r thro' - out the u - ni - verse dis -
E♭ E°7 B♭/F Dm/F F9 F7

25

Unison *mf*

played. Then sings my soul, my Sav-ior God, to Thee. How great Thou

Unison *mf*

B♭ E♭/F 25 B♭ E♭ B♭/D Gm7

mf

29

art! How great Thou art! Then sings my soul, my Sav-ior God, to

Cm7 E♭/F F7 B♭ E♭/F 29 B♭ E♭

Divisi CD: 56

Thee. How great Thou art! How great Thou

Divisi

B♭/D B♭ F7/C B♭/D E♭6 G7/D Cm F7

33
Solo
mp
And when I
art!
B♭2
E♭2/B♭
35
think that God, His Son not spar - ing, Sent Him to
F7/B♭
mp

39
die, I scarce can take it in; That on the cross, my bur - den glad - ly
Choir
Ooo
B♭2
E♭2/B♭
F7/B♭
B♭2
N.C.
p
CD: 57
bear - ing, He bled and died to take a - way my sin.
E♭/B♭
F9/B♭
B♭
E♭2/B♭
F7/B♭
B♭
B♭/A♭
mp

f Unison
44
When Christ shall come with shout of ac - cla -
f Unison
G sus
G
A m7
G/B
C
F/C
f
ma - tion And take me home, what joy shall fill my heart! Then I shall
mf
F
F♯°7
C/G
G
F/G
C
G
A m7
G/B
mf
48
CD: 58
bow in hum - ble ad - o - ra - tion, And there pro - claim: my God, how great Thou
48
C
F/C
F
F♯°7
C/G
G
F/G

52
ff Divisi
art! Then sings my soul, my Sav - ior God, to
Divisi
ff
C
F/G
52
C
F
ff
Unison
Thee. How great Thou art! How great Thou
Unison
C/E
Am7
Dm7
F/G
G7
56
Divisi
art! Then sings my soul, my Sav - ior God, to
Divisi
C
F/G
56
C
F

Thee. How great Thou art! How great Thou
C/E C/D C G7/D C/E F6 A7/E Dm G7
61
art! How great Thou art! How great Thou
C G7/D C/E F6 A7/E Dm G7
art!
C Db/C Eb/C C N.C.

Amazing Grace

with

Grace Greater than Our Sin

Arranged by Tom Fettke

CD: 59

Quietly ♩ = ca. 96

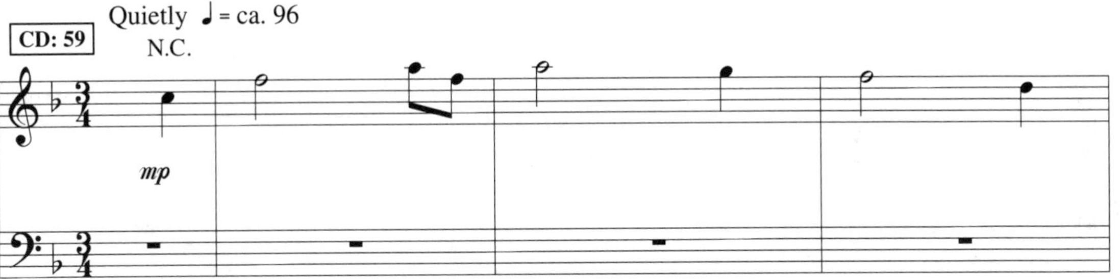

8 *"Grace Greater than Our Sin" (Johnson/Towner)

12
Grace that ex - ceeds our sin and our guilt,
12
C Dm/C C7 F Gm/F F Gm/F
16
Divisi
Yon - der on Cal - va - ry's mount out - poured,
Divisi
16
F C/F F C7 B♭/C C7 A/C♯ A7/C♯ Dm Dm/C
20
CD: 60
There where the blood of the Lamb was spilt.
20
Gm/B♭ Am Gm7 Am Gm/B♭ F/C C7 F

24
Grace, grace, God's grace,
Mar - vel - ous grace, in - fi - nite grace,
Grace, grace, God's grace,
Mar - vel - ous grace, in - fi - nite grace,
24
F
B♭/F
F
28
Grace that will par - don and cleanse with - in.
28
C7
C7
Am/C
C7
B♭/F
F
32
Grace, grace, God's grace,
Mar - vel - ous grace, in - fi - nite grace,
Grace, grace, God's grace,
Mar - vel - ous grace, in - fi - nite grace,
32
F
B♭/F
F

*Arr. © 1997 Birdwing Music. All rights administered by EMI Christian Music Publishing, PO Box 5085, Brentwood, TN 37024. All rights reserved. Used by permission.

48
saved a wretch like me! I
grace my fears re - lieved. How
Dm Dm7 F/G G7 B♭/C C7 Am/C
52
once was lost, but now am found; Was
pre - cious did that grace ap - pear The
F E♭6/F E♭/F F7 B♭2 B♭ F/A Gm7 C7sus C7 C/B♭
CD: 62 1st time
CD: 63 2nd time
56
blind, but now I see. 2. 'Twas
hour I first be -
F2/A F/A G9 F/C C7 N.C. F B♭/D C7sus C7

2
mf Divisi
62
lieved.
Thro' many - y dan - gers,
mf Divisi
F
F/E♭
D sus
D
G
D7
cresc.
mf
66
toils and snares I have al - read - y
Em
Em/D
C
G2/B
G/B
D7/F♯
G
Em7
A7
70
come.
'Tis grace hath bro't me
D
Em/D
D
D13
G
G2/B
G/B

74
safe thus far, And grace will lead me
C
Am7
D7sus D7
Em
Em
C♯
G
D
D7
78
home.
E♭
E♭
D
Cm
Cm
B♭
CD: 64
f Unison
When
f Unison
F
A
E♭
G
E♭
F
Fsus F
cresc.
f

84
we've been there ten thou - sand years, Bright,
84
B♭
B♭+
E♭
B♭
F
A
88
CD: 65
Divisi
ff
shin - ing as the sun, We've
Divisi
ff
88
G m
B♭
C
C 7
F
F
E♭
cresc.
92
no less days to sing God's praise Than
92
D♭
D♭9
D♭7
G♭
G♭
F
E♭m7
A♭sus
A♭
A♭
G♭
ff

96
decresc. poco a poco
when we first be - gun.
be - gun.
96
D♭/F
G♭M7
D♭/A♭
A♭7
D♭
decresc. poco a poco
100
mf
mf Grace, grace, God's grace. A -
100
D♭
D♭/C♭
G♭/B♭
D♭/A♭
104
decresc.
mp
maz - ing grace.
decresc.
mp
104
N.C.
D♭
decresc.
mp

When We All Get to Heaven

with

Sweet By and By
Just Over in the Gloryland

Arr. by Tom Fettke
and Richard Kingsmore

9
CD: 67
Fa - ther waits o - ver the way
pre - pare us a dwell - ing place
F Gm/F F Gm/F B♭/F F C/E Dm7 Am7/D Dm7 Gm7 Gm7/C C7
mf
13
there. In the sweet by and by, We shall
In the by and by,
F C F/C
meet on that beau - ti - ful shore.
the sweet by and
17
In the sweet by and
C7 F/C C7 F C/E

rit.
mp
by, We shall meet on that beau - ti - ful shore. We shall
Dm
Dm/C
B♭
C/B♭
F/C
C7
B♭/C
F
rit.
22
Faster - very bright ♩= ca. 126
CD: 68
meet on that beau - ti - ful shore.
F2/C
N.C.
E♭/F
B♭/F
f
mf Unison
I've a

26
*"Just Over in the Gloryland" (Acuff/Dean)
home pre - pared where the saints a - bide, Just o - ver in the glo - ry -
B♭ E♭/F B♭ B♭/F B♭ E♭/F B♭ B♭/F Gm7 C9 C7
mf Gospel 2-beat feel
30
CD: 69
land; And I long to be by my Sav - ior's side, Just
F F/C F B♭ E♭/F B♭ B♭/F B♭ E♭/F B♭ B♭/F
o - ver in the glo - ry - land. Just
Gm7 C9 F7 B♭

34
Divisi
o - ver in the glo - ry - land, I'll join the hap - py
o - ver, o - ver in the glo - ry - land, I'll join, yes join the hap - py
Divisi
34
B♭
Cm7/F
B♭
B♭/D
E♭
37
an - gel band,
an - gel band, Just o - ver in the glo - ry - land. Just
37
E♭/G
B♭
Gm7
C9
C7
F
40
o - ver in the glo - ry - land, There with the might - y
o - ver, o - ver in the glo - ry - land, There with, yes, with the might - y
40
B♭
Cm7/F
B♭
B♭/D
E♭

43
CD: 70
Unison
host I'll stand,
host I'll stand, Just o - ver in the glo - ry - land. When we
Unison
E♭ E♭/G B♭ Gm7 C9 F7 B♭
46
*"When We All Get to Heaven" (Hewitt/Wilson)
all get to heav - en, What a day of re-joic-ing that will
B♭ E♭/F B♭ B♭ E♭/F B♭ Gm Gm7 C7
50
be! When we all see Je - sus, We'll
F7 B♭ B♭9 E♭ E°7

CD: 71
sing and shout the vic - to - ry!
B♭/F B♭/D Cm7 E♭/F F7 B♭ B♭/A♭ G sus G
cresc.
f
55 March-like
mf Divisi
Sing the won - drous love of Je - sus; Sing His mer - cy
mf Divisi
55
C G7
mf
simile
59
CD: 72
and His grace. In the man - sions bright and bless - ed,
G7/B G C Am/G C Dm7 C/E C F F♯°7
59

63
Cut-time feel
He'll pre - pare for us a place. When we all get to
C/G C/E Dm7 Dm/G G7 C
63
C F/G C
Cut-time feel
heav - en, What a day of re - joic - ing that will be! When we
C F/G C Am D7 G7
67
CD: 73
all see Je - sus, We'll sing and shout the vic - to -
67
C C9 F F♯°7 C/G Dm7 F/G G7

72
ry! When we all get to
C
F/G
C
A♭
G♭/A♭
Fm/A♭
A♭7
D♭
G♭/A♭
D♭
heav - en, What a day of re - joic - ing that will be! When we
D♭
G♭/A♭
D♭
B♭m
E♭7
A♭7
76
all see Je - sus, We'll sing and shout,
D♭
D♭9
G♭
G○7
D♭/A♭

80
We'll sing and shout, We'll
D♭
A♭
D♭
80
E♭
D♭
cresc.
ff 84
sing and shout the vic - to - ry!
cresc.
ff
E♭m7
G♭
A♭
A♭7
G♭
A♭
A♭
84
D♭(no 3rd)
C♭
A♭
C♭
D♭
cresc.
ff
D♭
C♭
C♭
A♭
C♭
D♭
C
A♭
D♭
8va

Face to Face

with

Saved by Grace

Arranged by Tom Fettke

*A keyboard guide is provided on the accompaniment trax.

**Or sing the compete selection A cappella. At measure 28 sing the first two beats, then skip to the third beat of measure 32 and complete the arrangement as written.

7
When with rap - ture I be - hold Him, Je - sus
Face to face with my Re - deem - er, Je - sus
7
Christ who died for me?
Christ who loves me so!
11
mf
Face to face I shall be - hold Him,
mf
11
mf

Far be - yond the star - ry sky;
15
15
CD: 76 2nd time
Face to face, in all His glo - ry, I shall
CD: 75 1st time
1
2
mp
see Him by and by! by! And I shall
mp

*"Saved by Grace" (Crosby/Stebbins)

29
29
mf
33
And I shall see Him face to face, And
mf
33
decresc. and rit.
mp
tell the sto-ry– saved by grace.
mp
decresc. and rit.
mp

I Will Sing of My Redeemer

with

Love Lifted Me

Redeemed, How I Love to Proclaim It

Arranged by Tom Fettke

else could help, Love lift - ed me.
G/D
Em7
A7
A9
Am7/D
D7
13
Love lift - ed me! Love lift - ed
13
G
D7sus/G
G
C/G
G
G/B
Am7
G
Bm7
17
me! When noth - ing else could help,
C
E7/B
Am
Bm7
17
C
Em/C♯
G/D
Em
Cm6/E♭

CD: 79
21
rit.
Love lift - ed me. Love lift - ed
G/D
C M7/D
A m7/D
D 7
C2/G
G
G/B
C
G M7/D
rit.
*"I Will Sing of My Redeemer"
(Bliss/McGranahan)
Faster, in 3 ♩. = ca. 72
mf Unison
24
me. I will sing of my Re-
deem - er And His won - drous love to me; On the
D/G
C/G
D sus/G
E m7
A 9
D 7
A m7
mf

28
CD: 80
cru - el cross He suf - fered, From the curse to set me
G Em7 A9 D7 Am7 D7
free. Sing, O sing of my Re-deem - er, With His
G G/D G/B
32
C Am7 Bm Bm7 Em7
blood He pur-chased me. On the
Am7 D7 C/D D7 G

36
cross He sealed my par - don, Paid the
36 C Am7 Bm7 Em7
debt and made me free. Sing, O
f Divisi
Am4 D7 C/D D13 D7 G Am7 G/B
40
sing of my Re-deem - er, With His
Sing of my Re-deem - er, Sing, O sing of my Re-deem - er,
f Divisi
40 C Am7 Bm Em7
f

blood He pur - chased me; On the
He pur - chased me, with His blood He pur - chased me.

Am7 D7 C/D D G

44

cross He sealed my par - don, Paid the
He sealed my par - don, On the cross He sealed my par - don,

44 C Am7 Bm7 Em7

free.
debt and made me free, and made me free.
He paid the debt and made me free.

Am4 D7 C/D D13 D7 G C/G GM7 C/G G

*Arr. © 1997 Birdwing Music. All rights administered by EMI Christian Music Publishing, PO Box 5085, Brentwood, TN 37024. All rights reserved. Used by permission.

Divisi
60
child, and for - ev - er, I am. Re - deemed, re -
Divisi
B♭m7
E♭7
A♭
A♭7
D♭
B♭m7
deemed, Re - deemed by the blood of the Lamb. Re -
Cm7
Fm7
B♭m7
E♭7
D♭/E♭
E♭7
A♭
A♭/C
64
CD: 83
deemed, re - deemed, His child, and for - ev - er, I
D♭
B♭m7
Cm7
Fm7
B♭m7
E♭7

am.
A♭
A♭7/G♭
E7
69
Unison
Love lift - ed me! Love lift - ed
Unison
A
E7sus/A
A
D/A
A
A/C♯
Bm7
A
C♯m7
73
CD: 84
me! When noth - ing else could help,
D
F♯7/C♯
Bm
C♯m7
D
F♯m/D♯
A/E
F♯m
Dm6/F

ff Divisi
Love lift - ed me. Re -
Divisi
ff
A/E A M7/E D M7/E B m7/E E7 A
77
deemed, re - deemed, Re - deemed by the blood of the
77
D B m7 C♯m7 F♯m7 B m7 E7 D/E E7
ff
81
Lamb. Re - deemed, re -
A
81
D B m7

85
deemed,
His child, and for - ev - er, I
C♯m7
F♯m7
85
Bm
Bm/A
Bm/G♯
D/E
E13
am.
I'm re - deemed,
I'm re - deemed,
I'm re -
A
D6/A
A
D6/A
A
D6/A
89
deemed!
89
N.C.
A

To God Be the Glory

with

Revive Us Again

Arranged by Tom Fettke

12
CD: 86
glo - ry! Re - vive us a - gain.
Em
Em7
Am7
D13
D7
12
G
mf legato, no rit.
mf Unison
To
mf Unison
C/G
G
C/G
16
*"To God Be the Glory" (Crosby/Doane)
God be the glo - ry, great things He hath done; So
16
G
C/G
G
G/B
D7
G
G7

20
loved He the world that He gave us His Son, Who
20
C
G/D
Em7
A9
A7
D7
24
Divisi
yield - ed His life an a - tone - ment for sin, And
Divisi
24
G
C/G
G
D/F♯
G/F
28
CD: 87
f
o - pened the life - gate that all may go in. Praise the
f
28
C2/E
C/E
Cm6/E♭
G/D
D
G/D
D13
D7
G

32
Lord! praise the Lord! Let the earth hear His voice! Praise the
32
G Em A7 D7
f
36
Lord! praise the Lord! Let the peo - ple re - joice! O
36
Am Am/E D7 Em7 D/F♯ G
40
come to the Fa - ther thro' Je - sus, the Son, And
40
G C/G G D/F♯ G/F

44
CD: 88
give Him the glo - ry, great things He hath done.
44
C2/E
C/E
Cm6/E♭
G/D
D
G/D
D13
D7
G
decresc.
mf
49
We praise Thee, O God, for the Son of Thy
C2/G
49
G
C/G
G
mf
53
CD: 89
love, For Je - sus who died and is now gone a -
G
G/D
53
G
C/G
G/D
G/D
D sus

56
bove.
All
f
56
D
A♭
E♭
E♭sus
E♭
f
E♭7
59
glo - ry and praise to the Lamb that was slain, Who hath
59
A♭
A♭
E
E♭
A♭
A♭
E♭
63
f
borne all our sins and hath cleansed ev - ery stain. Hal - le -
63
A♭
D♭
A♭
A♭
A♭
E♭
E♭sus
E♭
A♭

67
lu - jah! Thine the glo - ry! Hal - le - lu - jah! A -
D♭/A♭ A♭ D♭/A♭ A♭
70
CD: 90
men! Hal - le - lu - jah! Thine the glo - ry! Re -
E♭ A♭ D♭/A♭ A♭ A♭/E♭ C/E Fm
73
vive us a - gain. Praise the
B♭m7 E♭13 E♭7 A♭ D♭/A♭ A♭

76
Lord!
Praise the Lord!
Hal - le - lu - jah! Thine the
76
A♭
D♭/A♭
A♭
glo - ry! Hal - le - lu - jah! A - men! Praise the
A♭
D♭/A♭
A♭
E♭
82
Lord!
Praise the Lord!
Let the peo - ple re -
82
E♭7
E♭
Fm7
E♭7/G

86
joice! O come to the Fa - ther thro'
A♭
86
D♭/A♭
A♭
90
CD: 91
Je - sus, the Son, And give Him the
E♭/G
A♭/G♭
90
D♭2/F
D♭/F
D♭m6/F♭
glo - ry, great things He hath done. Hal - le -
A♭/E♭
E♭
A♭/E♭
E♭13
E♭7
A♭

94
lu - jah! Thine the glo - ry! Re - vive
94
D♭/A♭
A♭
D♭
rit.
98
a tempo
us a - gain!
A♭/E♭
E♭
rit.
98
A♭
a tempo
A♭
8va

Take the Name of Jesus with You

with

Jesus Is the Sweetest Name I Know

Arranged by Tom Fettke

9
name,
O how sweet!
Hope of
D
D
F♯
F♯m7
G
E7
G♯
E
G♯
CD: 93
12
rit.
Faster ♩ = ca. 72
earth and joy of heav'n!
D
A
A13
A7
D2
C
D
Faster
15
mp
Take the name of Je-sus with you,
Child of sor-row and of
G2
C2
G
G
Am7
G2
B
G
B
C
D
C
C

CD: 94

19
woe.
It will joy and com - fort give you;
G/B
Am7
G
19
D
C/D
D
G
Em7
Take it then, wher - e'er you go.
Divisi
Pre - cious
Am7
G/B
CM7
C/D
D7
Gsus
G
23
name,
O how sweet!
Hope of earth and joy of
Pre-cious name,
O how sweet!
Divisi
23
C
G
G/B
D
G
G/F♯
Em7
A9

27
Pre- cious name,
O how sweet!
heav'n!
Pre- cious name,
O how sweet, how sweet!
Hope of
D7
D
G
G M7
B
C
C
Cm6
CD: 95
rit.
earth and joy of heav'n!
G
D
B m
D
D7
G
G
F
D♭
E♭
E♭7sus
E♭7
rit.
32
With a march feel
mf a tempo
At the name of Je- sus bow - ing,
Fall - ing pros- trate at His
mf
A♭
E♭
A♭
A♭
C
D♭
mf a tempo
accented

36
CD: 96
feet, King of kings in heav'n we'll crown Him
A♭/C B♭m4 A♭ E♭7 D♭/E♭ E♭ A♭ Fm7
When our journey is complete.
40
Precious name, Precious name, O how
B♭m7 A♭/C D♭M7 D♭/E♭ E♭7 A♭ D♭
legato
sweet! O how sweet! Hope of earth and joy of heav'n! Precious
A♭ A♭/C E♭ A♭ A♭/G Fm7 B♭9 E♭7

44
O how sweet! rit.
name,
Pre - cious name,
O how sweet, how sweet!
Hope of
A♭
A♭/C
D♭
Cm4
B♭m7
rit.
CD: 97
more rit.
earth and joy of heav'n!
A♭/E♭
Cm/E♭
E♭7
A♭
G♭/A♭
A♭7
more rit.
49
*"Jesus Is the Sweetest Name I Know" (Lela Long)
A little slower
Je - sus is the sweet - est name I know,
And He's
D♭
G♭
A♭/G♭
G♭
D♭2
D♭
D♭/F
A little slower

just the same as His love - ly name; And
Eb m4
Eb m7
Gb/Ab
Ab7
Gb/Db
Db
53
that's the rea - son why I love Him so.
Unison
O
Unison
Db
Gb
Ab/Gb
Gb
Db
Am6/Cb
Bb9
53
Je - sus is the sweet - est name I know.
56
Eb m7
Db/Eb
Gb/Ab
Fm/Ab
A°7
56
Bb m
Eb9

CD: 98
Je - sus is the sweet - est name I know.
E♭m
A♭
Fm
A♭
G♭
A♭
Fm
A♭
E♭m
A♭
D♭
59
Divisi
Je - sus is the sweet - est name I know, And He's
Divisi
D♭
G♭
A♭
G♭
G♭
D♭2
D♭
D♭
F
59
just the same as His love - ly name; And
E♭m4
E♭m
G♭
A♭
A♭7
G♭
D♭
D♭

63
that's the rea - son why I love Him so.
O
63
D♭
G♭
A♭/G♭
G♭
D♭
Am6/C♭
B♭9
rit.
Je - sus is the sweet - est name I know.
E♭m7
D♭/E♭
G♭/A♭
Fm/A♭
A °7
B♭m
E♭9
rit.
67
mp Slowly
Je-sus is the sweet-est name I know.
mp
67
E♭m/A♭
G♭/A♭
Fm/A♭
E♭m/A♭
D♭sus
D♭
mp Slowly